THOUGHTS OF

Family

I DON'T WANT TO GO

JERRY MILLER

ARPress

ILLUMINATING IDEAS.
EMPOWERING VOICES.

ARPress
45 Dan Road Suite 15
Canton MA 02021

Hotline: 1(800) 220-7660 Fax:
1(855) 752-6001

Ordering Information:
Quantity sales. Special discounts are available on quantity purchases by corporations, associations, and others. For details, contact the publisher at the address above.

Printed in the United States of America.

ISBN-13: Paperback   979-8-89676-234-8
          eBook   979-8-89676-235-5

CONTENTS

FOREWORD

As a young kid, I think I was part of the last generation to experience a viewing for a family member in the person's home.

Death of a loved one is difficult enough, but when you see them in the environment which held memories of laughter and games and apple pie; the comprehension of those times are now tainted with sorrow that haunted the memories of young kids that were not mature enough to experience such as a sad event.

The events depicted in this story are reminiscent of times more than 60 years ago when some young children were required to pay their last respects to departed family members and friends.

The sadness, the fear, the lack of comprehension inundated the very soul of the child, yet it was believed the very spirit of the departed would not be at peace until all family members acknowledge their love.

This is a story of the weakness of one child in a very desperate and unrelenting situation.

Chapter One

THE EARLY YEARS

In my early childhood I just loved to ride my scooter and tricycle. We had a long cindered walk on the side of our house and if that wasn't enough I could use the wide concrete walk alongside the street. It was fun; I'd make believe I was in the cab of a powerful Mack Truck pulling a trailer load of food for our local market. Sometimes I even attached my wagon and loaded up my dog. He didn't love it as much as I did…. he always tried to jump out but the movement made him very apprehensive, he couldn't wait until the ride was over. One day while riding my tricycle, I was near the back door of our house and I could hear my Mom crying, so I ran up the steps onto the porch and into the house, my Mom was standing with the telephone receiver in her right hand crying, anytime I saw my mom crying it really scared me. "Mom what's wrong" I shouted, standing there shaking…almost in tears myself, she immediately composed herself when she saw me standing there….brushing her fingers through my hair she said, "your Aunt Ceil died this morning", that was my Mom's sister (she was a short chubby, milky white skinned lady with her hair always tied back in a bun, always wearing little wire rim glasses and always wearing an apron), she was very sweet and always liked to pinch my chubby cheeks. At the time I didn't know what to do, I just stood there and waited for instructions, I guess from my Mom! I just didn't know what I should do or what should I say….Was it something I did? Something I said?….The first thing that came to mind was a couple weeks prior to her death me my mom and dad paid a visit to Aunt Ceil at her house. She was always jolly and loved to bake. Apple pies were her specialty and sometimes I think I was a chubby little kid because I could always eat more than one slice. After this little treat I can remember my Aunt Ceil going down to the basement to find an old newspaper that she wanted to give my Dad. Standing at the top of the stairs and looking down into the basement I echoed, "Aunt Ceil sure has a lot of junk down there"! I know now looking back, I hoped I didn't say something to make her die! Funny how when you're little you feel accountable for the misfortunes of people you love. My Mom tried to put my mind at ease and said she had a heart attack, of course at the time I didn't know what that was. My Mom tried to explain in a way that I could understand, "your Aunt Ceils heart was just too tired to go on"....I still couldn't figure it out and my obvious response at the time was…."why didn't she just give it a rest"? My mom said because…."she went to heaven to be with God and he will take good care of her". Well I was happy for that because her husband, my Uncle Jake got sick and had to leave her when I was only two and my final thought was that maybe when she's through dying we can visit her again.

The following day I was told we were going to Aunt Ceils house tomorrow night to see her. Now for a kid to get this oratory on death the day before and today learn we're going to pay a visit to see that person…I am very confused! "If she went to heaven, if she's now being taken care of by God, does that mean we got to go to heaven to see her? We never met God! What if he has other plans for her? Maybe they won't be home! Maybe they'll be at lunch. I was loaded with questions "Mom! How can we see her? She's in heaven and being taken care of by God, we don't know exactly where she lives, we don't know what she and God are doing, I mean, they may have plans"; Mother interrupted me, "honey, we will see your aunt someday and yes she is in heaven, and yes she is with God"….I just couldn't let it alone.."If she's in heaven and with God what's the purpose of our visit if she isn't home"?….Mom turned her head, looked at me with her soft compassionate brown eyes and said softly, "to see your aunt sleeping" "If Aunt Ceil is sleeping, she's not in heaven with God"…."but honey she is with God, her spirit is now with God….we will only see the likeness of what we remembered….you'll see tomorrow….everything will be ok". I know I was just a kid, but, when I think back, the whole thing was really beginning to give me the creeps.

Chapter Two

THE WAKE

The following day we arrived at Aunt Ceils house around 7pm. There were all kinds of cars parked all over the place and a line of people waiting to get into her house stretching two blocks….now could this be a surprise party for me (which was my immediate thought); otherwise I couldn't figure out why my mom and dad didn't tell me other people would be here. The only thing that was confusing about the whole arrangement was if it were for me why did we have to stand in line to get in, and why was it we had to stand at the end of the line? I hope she made enough apple pie to go around.

In line for 45 minutes, I had to go to the bathroom so I'm sure glad we're almost inside. We never had to wait this long to get into Aunt Ceils house before! By the time we get inside the apple pie will be all gone. At that time I was thinking if I knew any adult profanities that would depict how I felt about not getting a slice of her apple pie, but, I was a kid in the 40's, I didn't know any profanities.

Finally inside, what do I see, a whole bunch of people crying; flowers setting all over her living room and why were people standing around a wooden box? I wondered what they were looking at, they were so still, they were crying, and we were in line to see what was in the box. I was curious but somewhat apprehensive because there was something in that box that was either scary or very sad. As we approached the box I couldn't see anything at first because of the people in front of me. Their size obliterated my vision. Moving slowly forward, everything opened up, and there was my Aunt Ceil; lying very still; with a cross clinched in her hand I acknowledged her by calling her name; Aunt Ceil! She didn't answer….again, Aunt Ceil! Again she didn't answer so I touched her arm which felt stiff and unnatural and she didn't feel like the way I remembered, so again called her name, but, much louder and again she still didn't answer; my heart now pounding profusely, my hand tightly held in my mom's hand, I felt I was being held against my will, I wanted to get away, I wanted to run, to hide, I was so scared, I felt sick, I broke out of my mom's grip and screamed as I ran across the room, everyone looking at me, I was in a total panic, my heart beating so fast, so hard, you could literally see each beat on the surface of my white shirt, I just couldn't run fast enough, finally reaching the front door, I grabbed and turned the door knob releasing my incarceration from a house that was once filled with so much love and now perpetuated a dark vale of fear and sadness. I ran down the steps of the front porch and crawled through a small opening under the porch and hid. I wasn't there five minutes before I saw a shadow moving towards me, I stayed very still, very quiet, but the shadow came closer and closer, I couldn't move I was petrified, I whispered Aunt Ceil is that you? A little louder Aunt Ceil is that you ? Oooh, aaaah, I could now see it was spanky, our neighbors long haired Golden Retriever, panting and wagging his tail seemingly to know I needed his companionship. Spanky licked my cheek, and then laid down next to me, resting his chin on my leg, and starring at me with his big brown eyes, Spanky just gave me the comfort I needed.

I could hear my dad up on the porch calling me; he was almost frantic, I yelled back I'm here, under the porch, I could hear him say under his breath, thank god. What are you doing under there? I said Aunt Ceil scared me, hmmm, well lets go home son. It's all over ok? I was so glad we were leaving. I crawled out and got a hug from both mom and dad and said I never want to do that again! Let's go home, dad again echoed, we can talk about it in the morning if you like. I didn't want to talk about it at all, it scared me, all I could think of was seeing my Aunt Ceil in that box, thinking if we wanted to see her, is that how it will be from now on? Would we have to wait in line to get into the house? I don't want to go there ever again. I don't want to see people I love in a box.

Everyone was very quiet on the way home, except mom broke the silence with, "we have one more thing to do tomorrow, then it will be all over" now I'm thinking what's this all about? Do we have to go back to Aunt Ceils house? Mom! Do we have to go back to Aunt Ceils house? Dad said no son not to her house, but to where your aunt will be resting………..and where's that, I very curiously asked? She will be at a very quiet place with lots of trees and flowers, a very beautiful place. I wanted to know if she's still going to be in the box and what are they going to do with it? Mom interrupted by saying you'll see tomorrow son, everything will be ok. I remembered the last time being told everything would be ok, it was not ok it was a personification of having been introduced to fear, nothing beautiful, nothing that I could relate to, nothing I want repeated, nothing I ever want to do again. I just want to forget today ever happened, but, I can't I can't get it out of my mind; I keep seeing Aunt Ceil in that box, that big, brown, mahogany box.

Chapter Three

TIME FOR NIGHT NIGHT

We got back home around 9 o-clock and I remember being so stressed out having seen Aunt Ceil like I had never seen her or anyone else before, I was exhausted and yes ready to go to bed. I just wanted this day to be over, I just wanted to forget this day ever was. I never want to go through something like this again. I thought thank god for the golden retriever, I felt he really saved my sanity, if not my life.

I took a quick bath before heading upstairs to bed, the warm water felt so soothing and I almost fell asleep sitting in the tub. It really relaxed me. It felt so good, only to be brought back to my senses by a knock on the door; "are you ok son" it was my mom, "yes, I'm ok, I'm just sleepy"; "Don't fall asleep in the tub! Get out of the tub, and get dried off so you can get some rest, tomorrow's another busy day". I remember having forgotten about the following day and thinking it must have something to do with Aunt Ceil. I remember not wanting to do it again. "Mom do I have to go along tomorrow"? "I don't want to go, it scares me". "Son it's only a short visit and it's the final respects paid to someone you love. You'll be ok son; mom and dad will be by your side". I remember thinking I hate doing this and I'm beginning to hate Aunt Ceil.

Both Mom and Dad took me up to my room on the second floor, tucked me in, gave me a kiss and a hug, said good night, turned on a night light and went back down stairs. I couldn't get my mind off of tomorrow;

I really didn't want to go. I found myself just lying in bed staring at nothing in particular, except for a cedar chest against a wall about ten foot from the foot of my bed. Staring at the cedar chest reminded me of something and I tried remembering what it was. Oh Noooo! I yelled out. It's a box, Aunt Ceil is in that box! The lid's opening, Aunt Ceils going to come out, I tired to get out of bed, but the covers had me tucked in so tight, I felt like I was strapped in my own bed, I yelled out, Help! Help! Aunt Ceil is coming after me, I tried pushing the covers off, I can't do it, the covers are too tight, can't someone help me! I can't move, Help! Mom, Dad Help! Aunt Ceil is going to get me....Son! Son! Your ok it was only a bad dream! Shaking profusely, my forehead dripping with sweat, I now see my mom and dad on either side of me holding me tight, calming me down, trying to convince me that I was only dreaming, but, I know what I saw, and I don't want to go tomorrow! I hate Aunt Ceil! I never want to see her again!

Mom and Dad had no further response. The psychological damage this whole ordeal could cause may be irreversible and the respects paid to a loved one may obliterate any respect remaining for myself.

Chapter Four

THE BURIAL

The morning came, my dad woke me up, told me to get up, have some breakfast and start getting ready. Yes even with fear encompassing my total being, I still had to pay my final respects to someone I really don't know anymore, someone I don't want to know anymore. Aunt Ceil was someone that baked apple pie, someone that pinched my chubby checks and someone that gave me a hug and kissed my forehead, not someone that looked un-natural lying in a box. Why am I being forced to go today? Why are they doing this to me? I wanted to run away, I don't like it here anymore. I wanted to move far away. I felt sick, I thought I would vomit, I don't want to go, I don't want to pay any last respects.

I got out of bed, and as I walked out of my bedroom, my eyes focused on the cedar chest which to this day I swear contained the resurrected body of my Aunt Ceil. No longer did I walk perfectly parallel to that chest, a 180 degree radius was burned into the carpet which identified my path of departure. I hated my room, I felt the presence of something un-natural and I was made to deal with it.

I couldn't eat breakfast; I sat at the table and played with my food, I was too worried about what I'd be forced into doing today, what I'd be forced into seeing today and would Aunt Ceil be successful at penetrating my soul tonight in bed, after the lights go black, the air becomes still and my soul becomes a breeding place for the unscrupulous demon's that prowl what I once called my safe haven.

It seemed like I couldn't take long enough to get ready, I mean it seemed as though I got dressed so fast and now we have to go. I don't want to be part of this good bye, I no longer wanted to be Aunt Ceil's nephew, all I remember about that particular moment is wanting to go back to bed and hide under the covers quietly while my Mom and Dad back out of the driveway, but, unfortunately I was in the back seat of the car under a predetermined edict to accompany mom and dad to what they told me would be the cemetery. I remember during one of our many Sunday drives through the countryside and dad cracking a joke every time we past a cemetery, he'd say "Look over there, people are dying to get into that place". I would laugh never realizing that someday I'd have to deal with saying goodbye to someone. At one time my goodbyes were encapsulated in an old rickety floored house filled with the aroma of apple pie and a sweet little chubby lady standing at the front door, wearing an apron, kissing us all goodbye and ending with a pinch on my chubby checks. I wished it could be what it once was.

We arrived at the entrance to the cemetery; I remember a stone wall surrounded the grounds and a high wrought iron gate provided security and privacy to all those determined to be residents. A narrow road twisted and turned and wound it's way between beautifully sculptured monuments and very ornately positioned marble stones. At least 25 cars lined the narrow roadway, it's occupants standing around a gravesite waiting for the minister to recite a prayer appropriate to the deceased. I was fear stricken; I didn't want to walk over to where others were standing. What were they looking at? They were all looking down! What was I about to see? As we approached, the people seemed to open and provide a path to the center. I was shaking as the final four people stepped aside providing full view of the box which reminded me of the cedar chest. My heart now pounding uncontrollably, my hand my whole upper torso shaking, I wanted to run, why was my mom holding my hand so tight, everyone was crying, flowers were being thrown on to the box, but I envisioned flowers being thrown onto the cedar chest, I know Aunt Ceil is in there, she's in the cedar chest in my room, the box is now being lowered," where is it going? What will happen next"? "I want to get out of here"! I broke the grip of my mom's hand and just ran away from this grief stricken oasis, my dad running after me, gaining on me, grabbing me and holding on to me so tight I couldn't break away, I screamed, "let me go….let me go" but the iron grip of my dad's hands prevented me from running any further, I pleaded with him let me go," I'm afraid, I'm afraid, I don't want to be here I want to go home, I want to go home"! My heart pounding so profusely I thought the buttons on my shirt were about to pop off, but my dad's tight hug, and his soothing words eventually calmed me down as he carried me back to the car and I was once again reunited with my mom.

Chapter Five

THAT NIGHT

I remember it having been such a stressful day, especially for a young kid. The experiences I had to endure the last several days have created blisters inside my head that so blatantly continue to ooze a memory that feeds the nerve endings of my brain.

After arriving home, I found myself dozing off and on for the rest of the day. I was so exhausted!

Somewhere around eight that night I felt a hand on my shoulder and my mom's soft voice saying "son time to go to bed, you had a busy day and tomorrow it's back to school". I was so tired, so exhausted from the whole ordeal and I didn't feel like going to school tomorrow, but, it was Friday and I could look forward to the weekend. My room was upstairs, mom told me to go to my room put my pajamas on, hop into bed and both mom and dad would be up to tuck me in shortly. Climbing the stairs was an ordeal for such a tired body, I was barely able to lift my legs from one step to the next, I was so tired. Finally, I found myself in a small room adjacent to my bedroom, a room that was my bedroom before my big brother went into the navy and then got married. The room was illuminated by one 60 watt bulb and I found myself staring into a mirror, half awake and half asleep using my hand to brush my hair away from my forehead when my eyes refocused on my bedroom which was slightly illuminated by the one bulb in the spare room because the light on the night stand next to my bed had not yet been turned on. The illumination drew my attention to the cedar chest which seemed to cast an aura of darkness perpetuated by the shadow which was cast by the void of light. In this comatose state, I found my attention drawn to the cedar chest which was positioned against the wall several foot from the base of my bed. I seemed to freeze with curiosity, staring at the lid which appeared to be slightly moving back and forth and back and forth and back and forth and "Ahhhhhhhh"! "I don't want to go through this again, I don't want to go through this again, Aunt Ceil is coming to get me; Aunt Ceil is coming to get me"! My voice communicated fear, the lack of control, the harboring of demons as my mom and dad ran up the stairs coming to my aid, my body gyrating profusely, uncontrollably, my mom cradling my head while my dad held on to my arms finding it almost impossible to calm me down, my mom now crying, trying to console me, begging me to please calm down, "everything is ok mom and dad are here, nothing is here to hurt you". As fast as I lapsed into this state of transformation is as fast as I escaped back to the present. Shaking, sweating, confusion all encompassed my being at that moment and it was all caused by a belief that a young child must as well pay homage to a dear family member.

WHITE CLOUDS

What I see in a beautiful white cloud
Is serenity and peace
The purity in our heart
The love in our life
And goal in our future

TIME

If we could accept this moment in time,
The memories would be beautifully mine,
We would have no moments of regret,
We would forget about the time of fret.
But we do take for granted
This moment in time,
Thinking it will always last and
Forgetting it's not totally mine.
But for all the time, we had no time,
Cannot compare to the gift we shared,
If for only a brief moment in time.

BUSY

We are always busy
No time to talk or fuss
We are always busy
Doing things we think we must
We are always busy
No time to share a laugh
We are always busy
Living our days in the past
We are always busy
To take time out to kiss
We are always busy
To hold hands and reminisce
But we are not too busy as years go by
To wish we had a chance; at another try

FEELINGS

We all have feelings
Some good and some bad
A feeling is tricky
It makes us happy or sad
When we're happy we're giggly
We laugh at anything
A chore becomes simple
We display our profound dimples
When we're sad things are bad
They never do go our way
So the best thing that can happen
Is you send your love today!

MY BEAUTIFUL WIFE

Thank you my partner, my beautiful wife
Thank you for everything,
Our house, our children, our beautiful life
Without you, all of this
Would be immediately gone
Like without the songbird of morning
There would no longer be a song
To me you are perfect,
an Angel from above
A rose from heaven,
brought to me by a dove

MOM

Thank you Mom
For all you have done
You played an important part
To make my childhood fun

I'll never forget
All the things you did
The fun we had
When I was a kid

I'll love you forever
That's for sure
So please remember
This love will endure

DAD

Thank you Dad
For all you have done
You played an important part
Making my childhood fun

I'll never forget
All the things you did
The fun I had
When I was a kid

I'll love you forever
That's for sure
So please remember
This love will endure

MY LITTLE GIRL

When you were born
I could see
You would be the only
Little girl for me
Your little fingers
Your little toes
Not to forget
Your cute perky noise
The years they come
The years they go
The summers and winters
The pure white snow
The time moves by
So very fast
But my love for you
Will always last

MY LITTLE BOY

When years go by

so very fast

Some things I wish would always last

You've grown so fast

I can't believe

I wish that time

Could always be

If only for a moment in time

I would love

To tell the world

This little guy is mine

For the times I had no time

It will never be

Because you meant the world to me

I wish I could hold you

And kiss you goodnight

And tell you in our house

You will always be alright

But time is never still

It's always sneaks by
I would more than anything
Love to hear that little baby cry
No greater gift could I ever have had
Than to hear your Mom say
There's your dad
But I'm marches on
And thank God for one thing
The memories and pride
That you always bring

EVERYTHING

If reincarnation is a fact dear God
I ask for just one thing
Please give me back one more time
My Mom my Dad my everything
My beautiful Wife
All our children
None other can compare
No I don't want to
Change anything dear God
Except for one important thing
Please make me more mature to realize
I did have everything

OUR FLAG

It's hard to express how deeply I love this country of ours,

And how sacred they are that die in far places,

So we here at home can continue to enjoy

The freedoms, most people take for granted.

It's hard to express the pride I have in this great country,

When I hear the Star Spangled Banner,

And I place my hand over my heart,

And face the American Flag

It's hard to express what runs through my mind,

When I walk through Arlington Cemetery,

And I see each and every one proudly displaying the flag,

That followed great men and women,

To faraway places and back home,

To their final resting place.

It's hard to express what ran through my mind,

As I helped carry my Dad's flag draped coffin,

When vivid memories of long ago,

Had him carrying me.

I do understand why we love

This Brilliantly colored friend of ours.

It has been our confidant that stuck by us,

As a constant reminder,

Of those we love and cherish.

The serenity I feel from an ocean breeze,
will never surpass the serenity I feel
when I'm with you.

NONSENSICAL

At times things are hard to bear
Especially when you have no hair
People look with disbelief
They say cover your head with a dead leaf

Sometimes people don't exactly know
But try their darn to really snow
I can't imagine things going OK
When I wasn't raised that way

The days they come, the days they go
And I look forward to the crop I sowed
The greens that fill the earth layered field
Burst into color for my Mother who cooks the meals

Mother's meals do make me fat
I can't say I really like that
But it tastes so good I can't deny
So I won't say any more I won't even try!